ALONG THE SHORE

DISCOVERING JELLYFISH

Lorijo Metz

PowerKiDS press
New York

To T-Metz, the most unusual creature I know

Published in 2012 by The Rosen Publishing Group, Inc.
29 East 21st Street, New York, NY 10010

First Edition

Editor: Amelie von Zumbusch
Book Design: Kate Laczynski

Photo Credits: Cover iStockphoto/Thinkstock; pp. 4–5, 8, 9, 10, 15, 16, 19 Shutterstock.com; p. 6 © www.iStockphoto.com/ytwong; p. 7 Hemera/Thinkstock; p. 11 Roger Horrocks/Getty Images; pp. 12, 21 Tim (or Timothy G.) Laman/National Geographic Image Collection/Getty Images; p. 13 © www.iStockphoto.com/PlanctonVideo; p. 14 David Wrobel/Getty Images; p. 17 (top) Jeff Rotman/Getty Images; p. 17 (bottom) © www.iStockphoto.com/VMJones; p. 18 Paul Sutherland/Getty Images; p. 20 Pete Atkinson/Getty Images; p. 22 Tobias Bernhard/Getty Images.

Library of Congress Cataloging-in-Publication Data

Metz, Lorijo.
Discovering jellyfish / by Lorijo Metz. — 1st ed.
p. cm. — (Along the shore)
Includes index.
ISBN 978-1-4488-4997-0 (library binding)
1. Jellyfishes—Juvenile literature. I. Title.
QL377.S4M48 2012
593.5'3—dc22

2011000159

Manufactured in the United States of America

CPSIA Compliance Information: Batch #WS11PK: For Further Information contact Rosen Publishing, New York, New York at 1-800-237-9932

CONTENTS

FISH MADE OF JELLY?

In spite of their name, jellyfish are not really fish made out of jelly. They are not even fish! However, they do live in the ocean, as many fish do. The shiny, squishy bodies of some jellyfish do look a lot like jelly. However, their bodies are made mostly of water.

Jellyfish belong to one of the most common groups

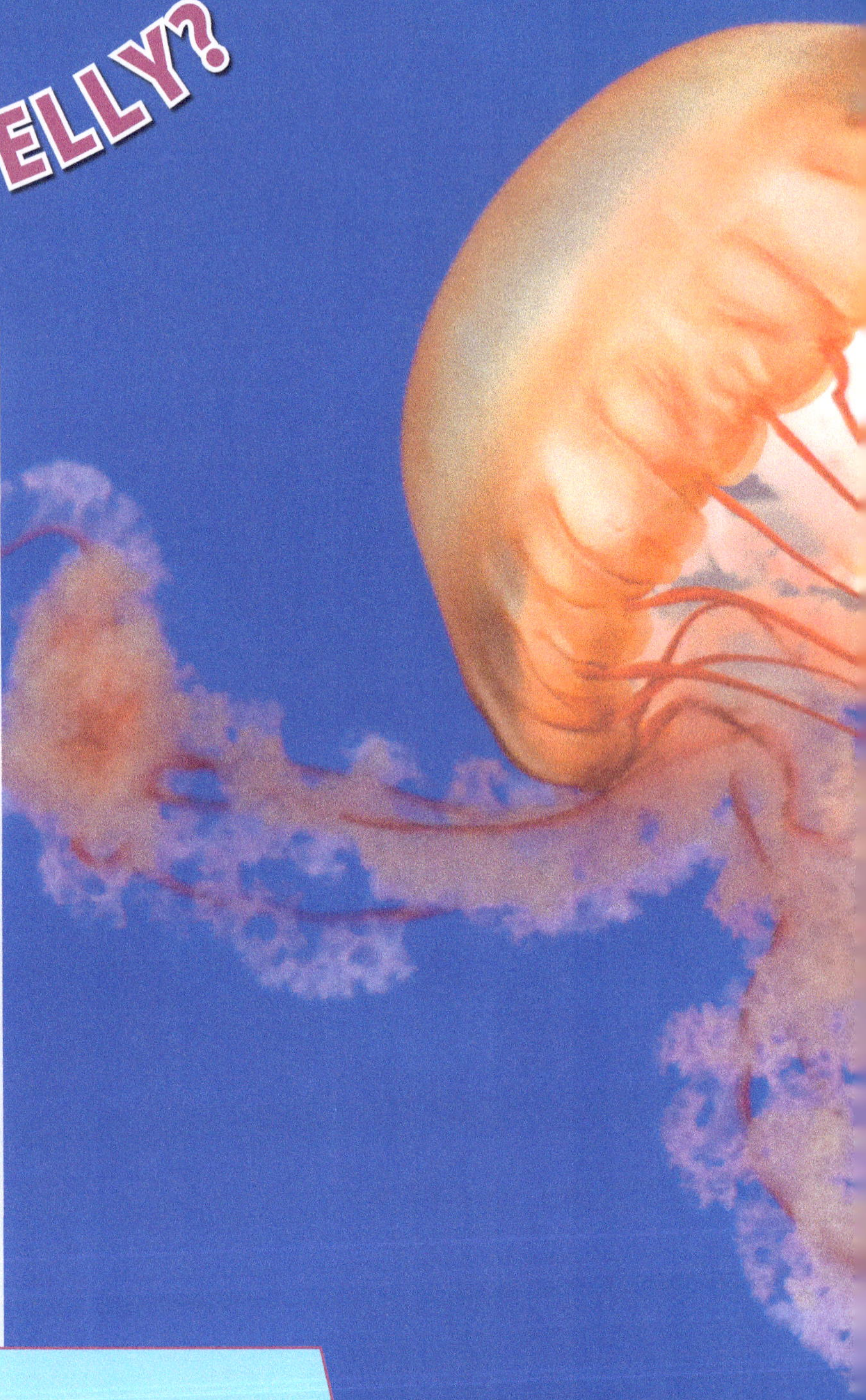

Many people find jellyfish strange looking but beautiful. What do you think about them?

of animals in the sea, **Cnidaria**. "Cnidaria" means "nettle." Nettles are plants known for their sting. Jellyfish sting, too. Their stings can be very painful. The stings of some jellyfish are even deadly. There are more than 2,000 **species**, or kinds, of jellyfish.

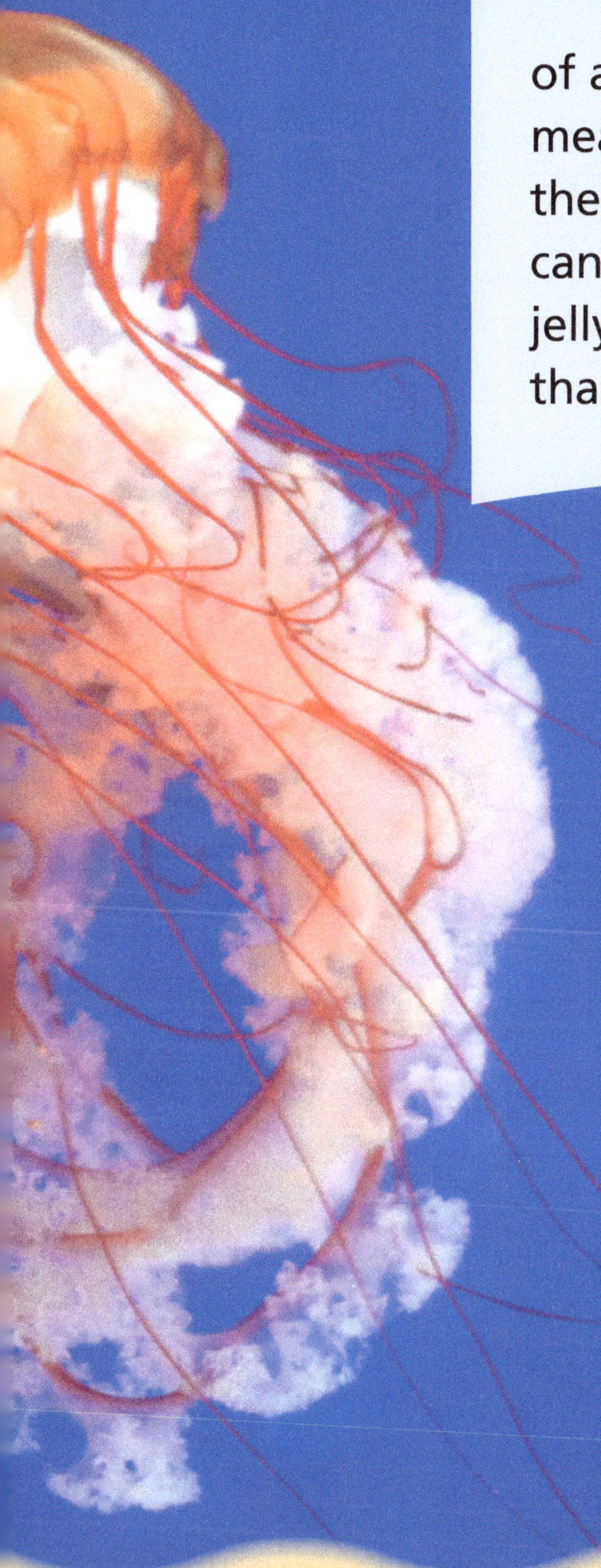

JELLYFISH FACT

Jellyfish have been around for a long time. Today's jellyfish look much the same as those that swam the oceans millions of years before the dinosaurs.

JELLYFISH BODIES

Jellyfish tend to look like umbrellas or giant mushroom caps. They float quietly through the water. A jellyfish's body is called a bell. Jellyfish move forward by squeezing water through their bells. This pushes them forward, much as the air rushing out of a balloon makes it zoom around.

JELLYFISH FACT

Jellyfish are full of water. The water supports their bodies much as air fills a balloon. Without water, their bodies would cave in and they would die.

Jellyfish breathe through their thin outer skin. They do not have lungs, as people do, or gills, as fish do.

Many jellyfish have such thin skin that you can see through parts of their bodies.

Ribbonlike stinging arms, called **tentacles**, and long tubes, called **oral arms**, hang beneath most jellyfish bells. Jellyfish use their tentacles to catch food. The oral arms bring food to their mouths. Jellyfish mouths are at the bottoms of their bells.

Some jellyfish have eyespots. These are spots on the edges of the jellyfish's bell that sense light.

LIGHTS IN THE SEA

If you look out over the ocean on a dark night, you might see green or blue lights in the water. What makes these lights? It could be jellyfish! Some species of jellyfish produce light in their bodies. One jellyfish that does this is the crystal jellyfish.

These jellyfish are crystal jellyfish. The parts of their bodies that make light are around the edges of their bells.

Crystal jellyfish live in the Pacific Ocean. They are found off the coast of North America from Alaska to Baja California.

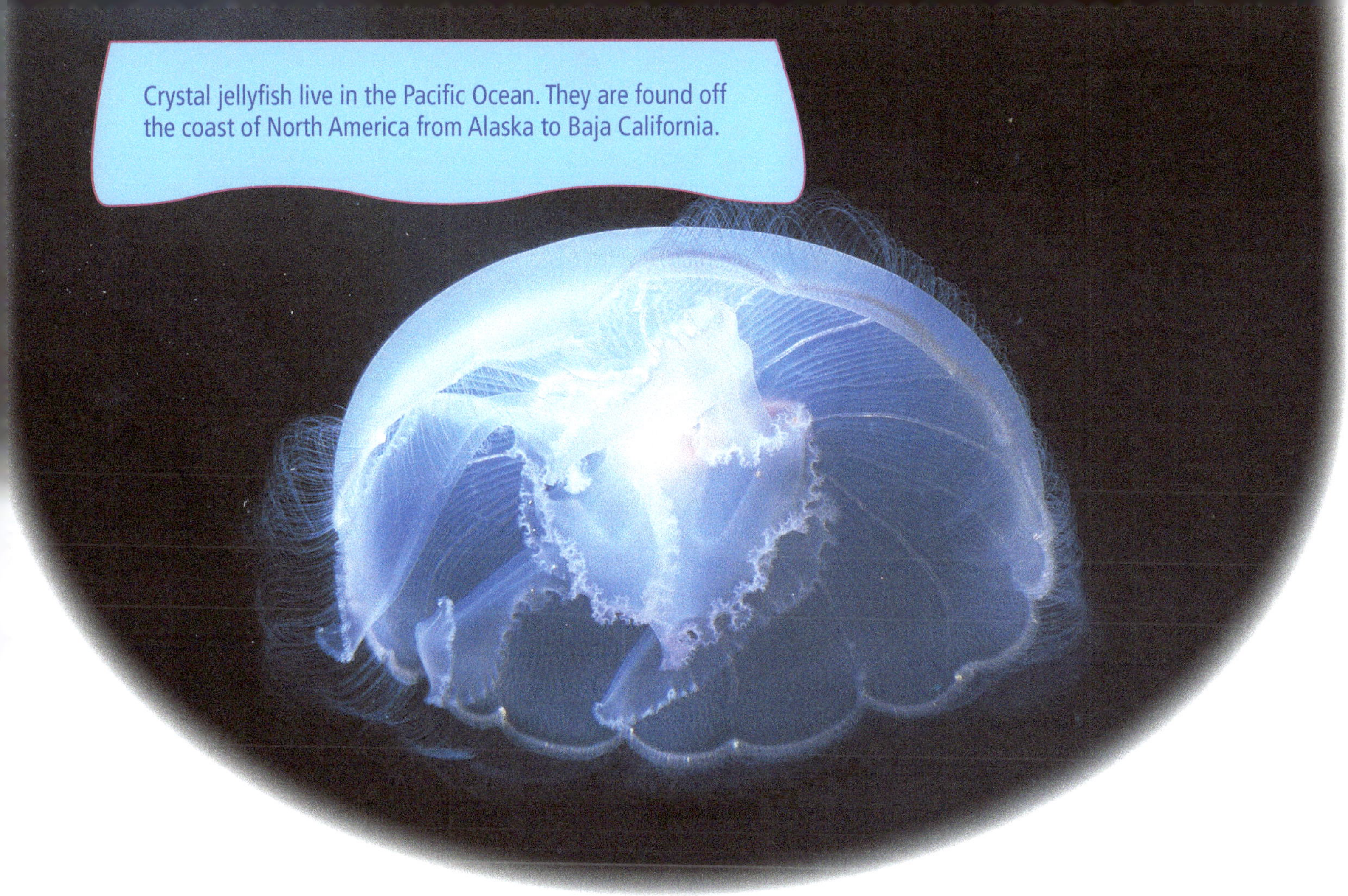

There are several reasons jellyfish produce light. Jellyfish are slow swimmers. They often drift along with the ocean. Fish and other animals that jellyfish eat are drawn to their light. Once they come near, jellyfish can eat them. Jellyfish also use light to draw other jellyfish to them when they are ready to have babies.

OUCH! THE STING OF A JELLYFISH

Jellyfish catch their dinner using **nematocysts**, or stinging cells. The nematocysts may be on their tentacles, oral arms, or mouths. Each nematocyst has a tiny dart wound up tightly inside it. When a fish brushes against the nematocyst, the tiny dart shoots out. The dart is filled with **poison**.

This jellyfish is a black sea nettle. These jellyfish sting things with their tentacles. Their tentacles can grow to be 25 feet (8 m) long.

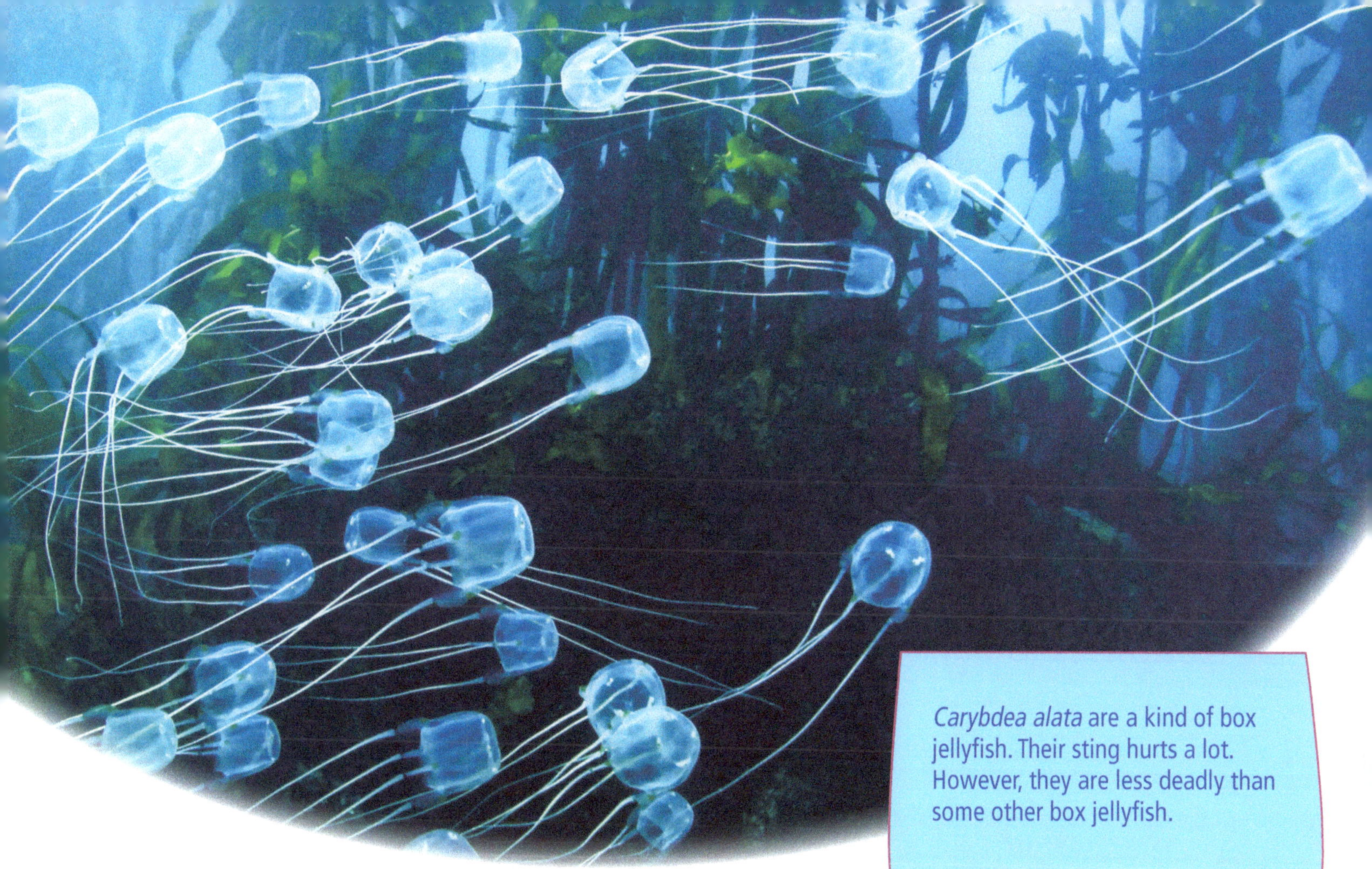

Carybdea alata are a kind of box jellyfish. Their sting hurts a lot. However, they are less deadly than some other box jellyfish.

The poison makes the fish unable to swim. Sometimes, it even kills the fish. A jellyfish may sting a fish with hundreds of its nematocysts.

For people, most jellyfish stings are simply painful. However, the sting of certain kinds of box jellyfish can kill a person in under 15 minutes. These jellyfish live off the coasts of Australia.

ALL SHAPES AND SIZES

One of the smallest species of jellyfish is the thimble jellyfish. These tiny glowing jellyfish are only 1 inch (2.5 cm) wide. They are known for their stings. They can leave swimmers with a red rash, or breakout, called sea bather's eruption.

As you might guess, the upside-down jellyfish lies upside down on the ocean floor. Its moving tentacles look like seaweed. Plantlike animals

This upside-down jellyfish is in the waters off the coast of Belize. Upside-down jellyfish can be found in warm waters in many parts of the world.

Fried egg jellyfish are also known as Mediterranean jellies. They live in the Atlantic Ocean and the Mediterranean Sea.

called **algae** live inside the tentacles.

Upside-down jellyfish live in waters close to shore. They get lots of sunlight there. Algae make the food they need from sunlight. The algae inside upside-down jellyfish share the food they make with the jellyfish, too.

JELLYFISH FACT

The lion's mane jellyfish is the largest jellyfish. It can be up to 8 feet (2 m) wide. Its long tentacles look like a lion's mane. The tentacles can grow to be more than 100 feet (30 m) long.

HOW DO JELLYFISH GROW?

Female jellyfish produce thousands of eggs. They carry the eggs for a few days before the babies inside them break out. Baby jellyfish are called **larvae**. They look nothing like their parents. Only a few live to reach the ocean floor.

These are moon jellyfish polyps. The brownish ones are starting to break and become young jellyfish. A jellyfish that just split off from a polyp is called an ephyra.

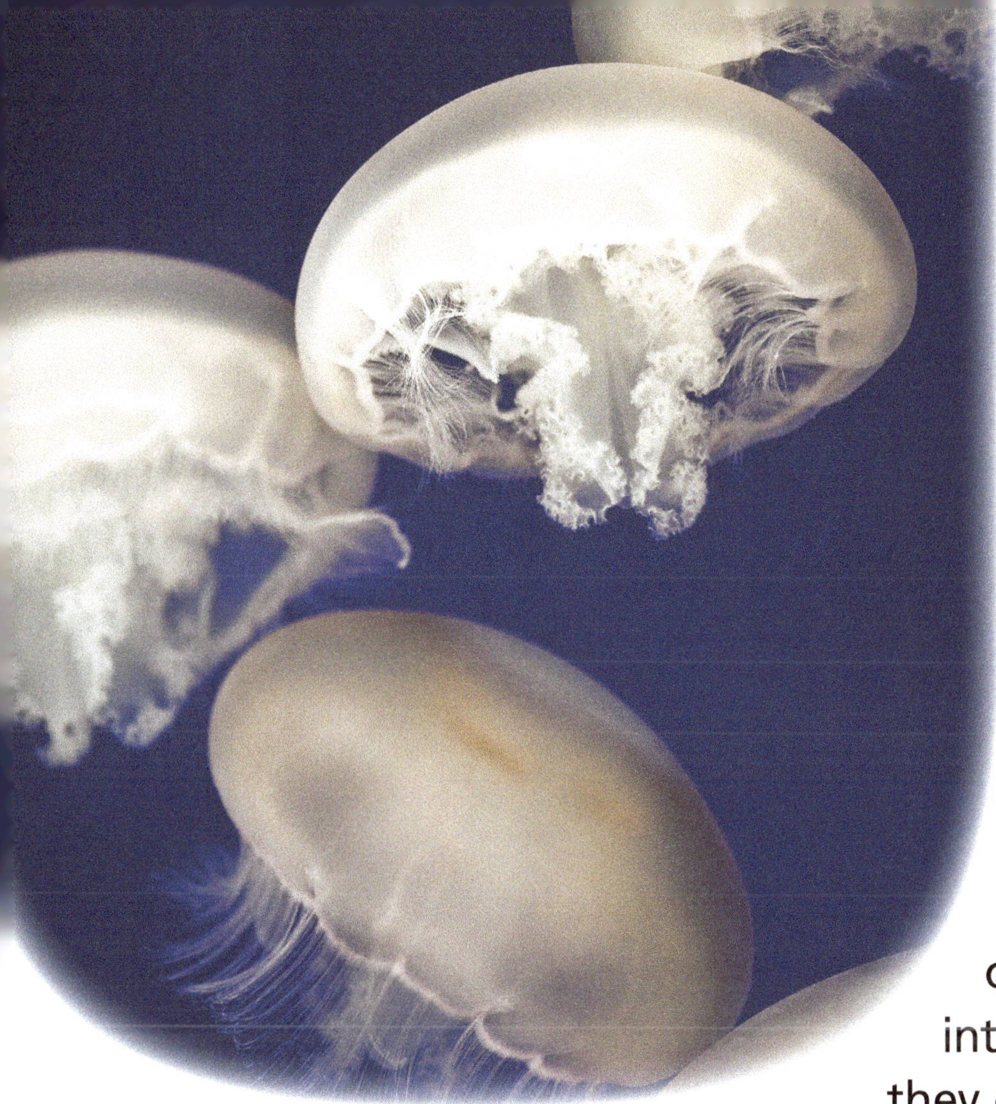

These jellyfish are moon jellyfish medusas, or adults. Moon jellyfish are among the most-studied kind of jellyfish.

There, the larvae fix themselves to rocks or seaweed and turn into **polyps**. As polyps, they grow long stems that end in a ring of tentacles around one mouth.

After a few weeks or months, the top part of the polyp begins to break into layers. Tiny jellyfish break off and float away from the polyp. They grow into **medusas**, or adults. In time, they will have their own babies.

WHERE ARE ALL THE JELLYFISH?

Jellyfish live in every ocean of the world. Some live in warm tropical waters. Others are found in the cold waters of the Arctic Ocean. Some live along coasts, while others live very deep in the ocean.

Jellyfish often drift where the ocean takes them. When the ocean pulls a huge group together, this is called a bloom. A bloom might have

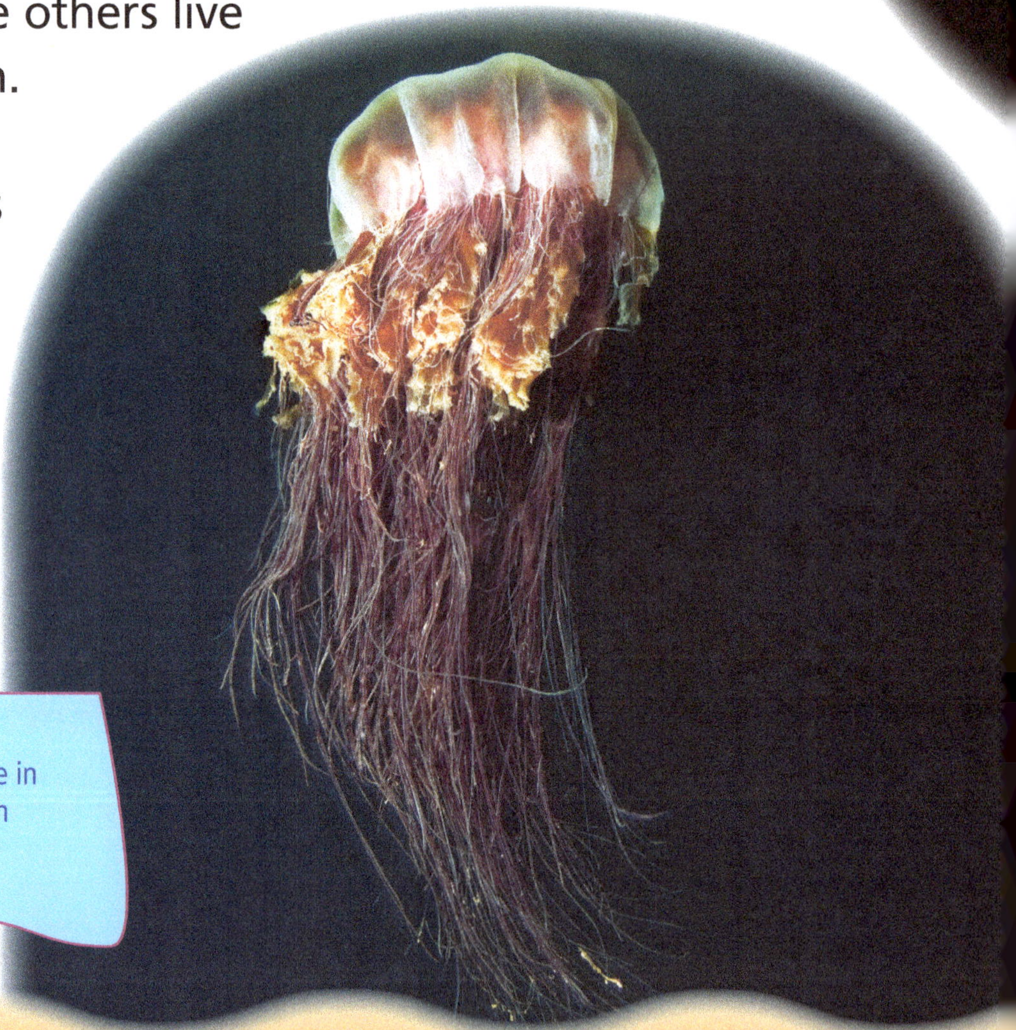

Lion's mane jellyfish, such as this one, live in the cold waters of the Arctic Ocean, North Pacific Ocean, and North Atlantic Ocean.

Penicillate jellyfish live off North America's Pacific coast. They are also called red-eye jellyfish and bell-shaped jellyfish.

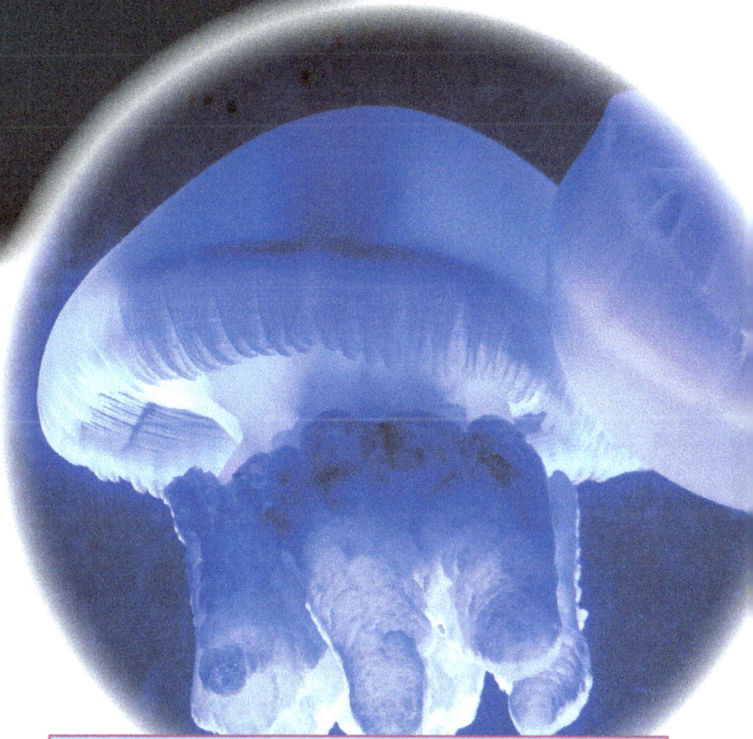

Blue blubber jellyfish are commonly seen off the coasts of eastern and northern Australia.

as many as 100,000 jellyfish. Blooms also happen for other reasons. On the darkest night of the month, thousands of box jellyfish come close to shore in Hawaii to **mate**, or have babies. While blooms are interesting to see, they are a danger to swimmers!

WHAT DO JELLYFISH EAT?

Jellyfish eat fish and other animals that live in the sea, such as shrimp. Most jellyfish wait for their prey, or food, to come to them. Species that feed on larger prey tend to have long tentacles covered with many nematocysts. First, they sting their prey so they cannot swim. Then they slowly bring the prey to their mouths through their oral arms.

This box jellyfish has caught a fish. You can see another fish in its stomach. This box jellyfish is one of the deadly ones that live near Australia.

This jellyfish is a sea nettle. Sea nettles eat plankton, small fish, and other jellyfish.

JELLYFISH FACT

Jellyfish have only one opening, their mouth. Not only do they eat with their mouth, they also return waste to the sea through their mouth.

Other jellyfish eat **plankton**, or tiny plants and animals that live in the sea. These jellyfish tend to have sticky skin and tentacles with tiny hairs. The hairs push the plankton past the jellyfish's mouth, trapping it on the sticky skin.

JELLYFISH PREDATORS AND LITTLE FISH

Jellyfish may have deadly stings, but many animals still eat them. Giant leatherback sea turtles eat almost nothing else. Crabs and moonfish eat them, too. Sea slugs have special coatings that keep jellyfish stings from hurting them. In fact, sea slugs save the jellyfish

Several kinds of sea turtles eat jellyfish. This green sea turtle is about to take a bite out of a jellyfish.

This crab is carrying an upside-down jellyfish on its back. The jellyfish hides the crab and will sting anything that tries to eat the crab.

nematocysts on their backs. They use them to sting other predators.

Jellyfish have a special coating to keep from being stung by their own nematocysts. Tiny fish often swim beneath jellyfish. They cover their bodies with the special coating by rubbing against the jellyfish. The coating keeps them safe from the jellyfish's sting. The jellyfish keep the fish safe from other predators, too.

JELLYFISH AND PEOPLE

Jellyfish is a prized food in many Asian countries. Jellyfish are high in **protein**. Protein is something people need to live. There are many jellyfish in the ocean. This makes some people think that jellyfish would be a good food supply for the world's hungry people.

This diver is looking at a jellyfish. The light he is holding helps him get a good look at the jellyfish.

To see live jellyfish without being stung, visit an aquarium, such as Shedd Aquarium, in Chicago, Illinois. There you can see underwater wonders, such as the moon jellyfish, from behind the safety of a glass wall.

GLOSSARY

algae (AL-jee) Plantlike living things without roots or stems that live in water.

Cnidaria (ny-DER-ee-uh) A group of boneless water animals that catch their food by stinging it.

larvae (LAHR-vee) Animals in the early period of life in which they have a wormlike form.

mate (MAYT) To come together to make babies.

medusas (mih-DOO-suz) Adult jellyfish.

nematocysts (NEH-muh-tuh-sists) The stingers of some types of animals.

oral arms (OR-ul AHRMZ) Long body parts that certain sea animals use to bring food to their mouths.

plankton (PLANK-ten) Plants and animals that drift with water currents.

poison (POY-zun) Something that can cause pain or death.

polyps (PAH-lips) An early stage of a jellyfish's life.

protein (PROH-teen) An important element inside the cells of plants and animals.

species (SPEE-sheez) One kind of living thing. All people are one species.

tentacles (TEN-tih-kulz) Long, thin growths on animals that are used to touch, hold, or move.

INDEX

WEB SITES

Due to the changing nature of Internet links, PowerKids Press has developed an online list of Web sites related to the subject of this book. This site is updated regularly. Please use this link to access the list:
www.powerkidslinks.com/alsh/jelly/